OmniMeta
Mindfulness

Power Up, Zone In, and Own Your Day—No Matter What Comes Your Way

OmniMeta Mindfulness

Copyright © Sukant Ratnakar
Hardcover ISBN: 978-1-998440-09-2
Paperback ISBN: 978-1-998440-08-5
Audio ISBN: 978-1-998440-10-8
First Edition: 2024

Illustrations by Jovial Jasmine
Cover image courtesy of Freepik.com
For permissions or inquiries, please contact publisher

Quantraz Inc.
SUOL Center, Canada
Email: hello@quantraz.com
Website: www.quantraz.com
Printed in India

Behind the Words

In a world buzzing with distractions and constant demands, OmniMeta Mindfulness is your guide to finding clarity, balance, and strength. It's about tuning into your body, thoughts, senses, and energy, bringing together practical tools to align your inner and outer worlds. Through the BOSE Framework, mindfulness becomes part of your everyday flow, helping you navigate life's challenges with calm and focus.

Life feels chaotic—endless information, nonstop notifications, and the pressure to juggle everything. Mindfulness cuts through the noise, bringing your mind back to what truly matters. It helps reduce stress with simple practices like deep breathing, grounding you in the present and pulling you away from yesterday's weight or tomorrow's worries.

But it's more than stress relief—it boosts focus, balances emotions, and helps you respond thoughtfully rather than impulsively. Mindfulness enriches your connections, well-being, and ability to be fully present.

At its core, mindfulness means being here, fully. Whether you're working, relaxing, or simply living, it's about finding joy in the small moments and deepening your bond with yourself and those around you.

— Sukant Ratnakar

"Mindfulness: Simplify the chaos and focus on what truly matters."

Content Roadmap

Mastering the Present Moment

We live on the edge of time, and it's easy to slip into the past or future without realizing it. The real challenge isn't drifting—it's having the control to snap back to the present when we need to. But first, do we even know where our mind is wandering? OmniMeta is all about building that awareness and mastering the ability to be present.

"Control is guiding the mind back to the present."

Chapter 1

The Heart of Mindfulness

What is Mindfulness?

Mindfulness is about being fully present. It's the practice of paying attention to what's happening right now—your thoughts, emotions, body, and surroundings—without any judgment. Instead of getting caught up in past regrets or future worries, mindfulness brings you back to the here and now.

"Are you really here, right now?"

Engaging with the Moment

When you practice mindfulness, you become aware of your thoughts and feelings without letting them control you. It's not about shutting off your mind; it's about creating space between you and your reactions. Observing each moment with an open mind helps you find calmness in everyday life.

"See your thoughts without being them."

Mindfulness in Everyday Actions

Mindfulness doesn't have to be complicated. It can be as simple as taking a breath before speaking, savoring the taste of your food, or feeling the ground beneath your feet when you walk. Every moment is an opportunity to connect to the present, and these small mindful moments make a big difference in how grounded and balanced you feel.

"Small mindful moments add up."

Cultivating Mindfulness: A Daily Practice

Like any skill, mindfulness gets easier the more you practice. By making it a daily habit, you build deeper self-awareness and emotional balance. Over time, mindfulness becomes second nature, helping you navigate life with greater peace and clarity.

"Practice presence; feel the difference."

Notes

Chapter 2

OmniMeta Mindfulness: The Journey Within

OmniMeta Mindfulness

Welcome to the start of your OmniMeta Mindfulness journey—a process to help you connect deeply with yourself and find balance in your body, mind, senses, and energy.

So, what is OmniMeta Mindfulness? Think of it as a guided path through your inner world. Each step moves you with intention toward greater awareness, balance, and focus.

"Find balance by turning inward."

Breaking Down "OmniMeta"

"OmniMeta" might sound complex, but it's actually simple. "Omni" represents the all-encompassing nature of this practice—connecting with all parts of who you are. "Meta" is about going deeper, exploring what's beneath the surface. Together, OmniMeta Mindfulness is an exploration of yourself, with each Stage bringing a unique role and direction.

"Explore deeper layers of you."

A Gentle Flow of Focus

What makes this approach special is how it plays with focus—flowing gently, like waves rising and falling. Sometimes you'll sharpen your focus, zooming in. Other times, you'll soften your awareness, letting things be. This rise and fall lets you explore different layers of mindfulness, guiding you from a broad perspective to deeper concentration—and then back out.

"Flow with focus, rise with awareness."

The Flexibility of OmniMeta

OmniMeta Mindfulness is flexible and adaptable. Each step builds on the last, helping you connect with how you feel, think, and exist in the moment. It's about balance, clarity, and being present. As you practice, you'll discover more alignment within yourself—where your breath, body, and thoughts move in harmony.

"Find your balance; live in harmony."

A Roadmap to Presence

Think of this journey as a roadmap guiding you to a more aligned version of yourself. Your breath, your body, and your thoughts all moving in a direction that feels uplifting and just right for you. This is your time to tune in, realign, and balance your energy, so you can be fully present in your life.

"Tune in to who you are."

Mindfulness: The Heartbeat of OmniMeta

So why call it "mindfulness" when it also involves meditation, intention setting, reflection, and visualization?

Mindfulness goes beyond just staying in the present. It's about being fully aware and engaged in whatever you're doing—whether that's focusing on your breath, setting an intention, reflecting on your thoughts, or visualizing your future. Think of mindfulness as the umbrella that brings all these elements together, allowing you to be fully conscious and connected—without judgment.

"Mindfulness: more than a moment."

Why Mindfulness Matters

Why is mindfulness so important? Because the present moment is the only reality we can actively engage with and control. We can't change the past or predict the future, but we can guide our actions and intentions toward what lies ahead. Reflection and visualization add depth and meaning, letting you learn from the past while shaping your future.

"Live now, guide what's next."

Building Balance Through Practice

As you move through meditation, reflection, mindfulness, and visualization, you build strength and control over your mind. Each Stage enhances your ability to be mindful, bringing balance and clarity to your experiences. Even though OmniMeta Mindfulness uses a variety of techniques, they all connect back to one thing—mindfulness.

"Balance starts with focus."

A Unified Flow

Whether you're meditating, reflecting, setting a daily intention, or imagining your future, it's about being fully here and now. OmniMeta Mindfulness is a unified flow that guides you through layers of your body, mind, senses, and energy—helping you move forward with purpose and presence.

"Fully here. Fully now."

Chapter 3

The Foundations of OmniMeta

The Foundations of OmniMeta Mindfulness

OmniMeta Mindfulness is built on two fundamental building blocks: The BOSE Framework and the MetaCycle. Each serves a unique role in guiding you toward deeper awareness and presence, seamlessly working together to create a balanced, mindful flow.

"Foundation shapes focus; build with purpose."

OmniMeta Mindfulness Core Components

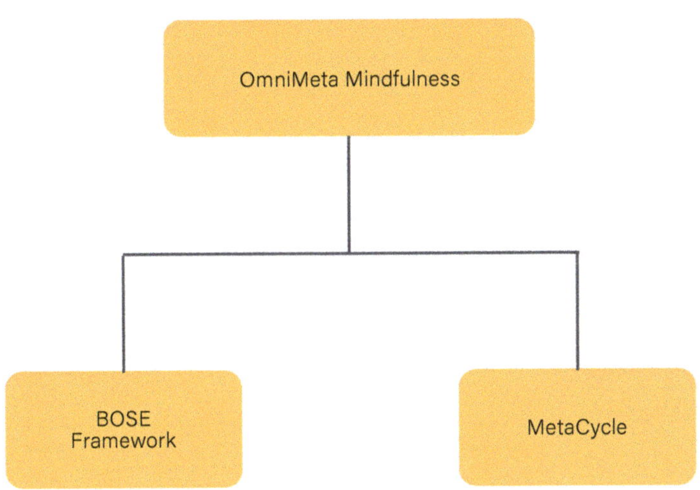

Notes

Chapter 4

The BOSE Framework: A Closer Look

The BOSE Framework

Let's dive into the core elements of OmniMeta Mindfulness. First, the Omni Element comes through the BOSE Framework, which focuses on four key pillars: Body, Observations, Senses, and Energy.

Your **Body** grounds you, creating awareness of how you physically feel. **Observations** offer insight into your thoughts and emotions—a gentle inward look. **Senses** connect you to the world, tuning into what you hear, see, touch, taste, and smell. And **Energy** aligns your overall well-being, letting you notice how energy flows in different areas of your life.

"Feel. Observe. Sense. Energize."

The MetaCycle

Then there's the Meta Element—known as the MetaCycle. It's the rhythm guiding your practice, creating a natural flow as you move through the BOSE Framework.

The MetaCycle comes in two forms: Macro and Micro. The Macro MetaCycle covers the big picture—like the warm-up and cool-down of your practice. Think of it as opening and closing the door to your mindfulness journey.

"Flow from big picture to detail."

The BOSE Framework: A Path to Mindfulness

The BOSE Framework is the foundation of OmniMeta Mindfulness, focusing on four core elements: Body, Observations, Senses, and Energy. It's a way to break down and explore our experiences, one step at a time.

"Mindfulness begins when we explore each layer of our being."

BOSE Framework

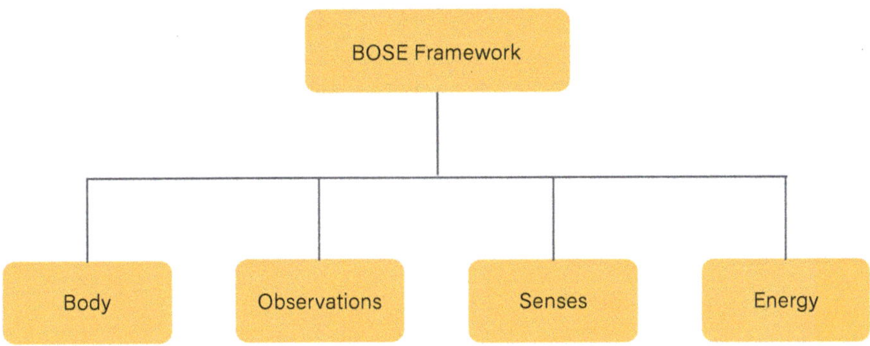

Body

We start by connecting with our body—its posture, tension, and areas of ease. This grounds us in the present moment, helping us stay rooted in our physical self.

"Stay grounded. Feel your body."

Observations

Next, we shift focus to our thoughts and emotions. What's going on in your mind? Are you feeling calm, anxious, scattered? Simply observe without trying to change or judge.

"Observe your thoughts; let them be."

Senses

Then, we tune into our senses—the sounds, sights, textures, tastes, and smells around us. By doing this, we add more depth to the present moment, making each second richer.

"See the world through your senses."

Energy

Lastly, we check in with our energy—physically, mentally, emotionally, spiritually, and socially. Where is your energy flowing freely? Where does it need balance? Notice what feels in tune and what needs realignment.

"Balance your energy, find your flow."

Notes

Chapter 5

The MetaCycle: Your Mindfulness Rhythm

MetaCycle

The MetaCycle is a core process within OmniMeta Mindfulness, composed of six stages designed to enhance mindfulness and personal growth. It begins with **Meditation** to center the mind, followed by **Intent Setting** to establish clear goals. **Reflection** encourages self-awareness, while **Mindfulness** helps maintain present-focused attention. **Visualization** fosters mental imagery of desired outcomes, and **Outcome Reflection** assesses how actions align with intentions. Together, these stages form a continuous loop, supporting self-improvement and deeper awareness in both personal and professional life.

Metacycle

MetaCycle
Meditation
Internet Setting
Reflection
Mindfulness
Visualization
Outcome Reflection
Stage 1
Stage 2
Stage 3
Stage 4
Stage 5
Stage 6

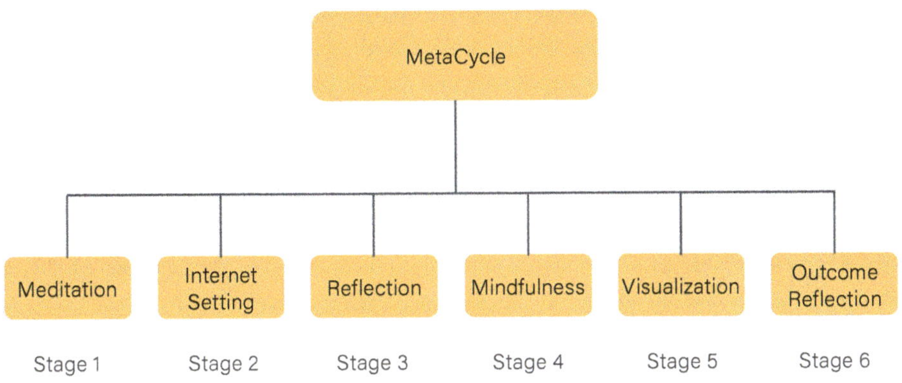

The Timeflow Continuum

In "Timeflow Continuum", a sequence of color blocks visually represents the flow of time: "Distant Past" (red), "Recent Past" (yellow), "Present Moment" (gray), "Near Future" (light blue), and "Distant Future" (blue). Arrows connect these time periods, illustrating the continuous, dynamic relationship between them, with the "Present Moment" as the pivotal point. The concept emphasizes how our past experiences shape our future, while highlighting that the present is where choices are made and action occurs, directly influencing what lies ahead.

The Time flow Continuum

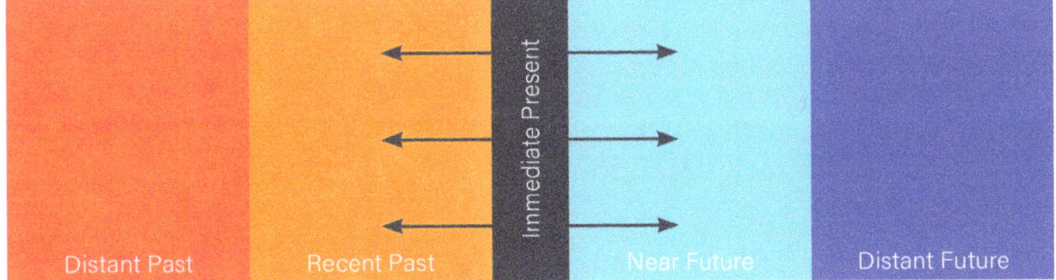

Flowing Through the MetaCycle

Let's dive into the MetaCycle—a gentle wave that guides your focus to rise and fall. Picture it: a smooth, natural flow, like riding a wave that carries you effortlessly from one state of awareness to the next."Ride the flow, let your focus find its rhythm."

The Flow of MetaCycle: Aligning Past, Present, and Future

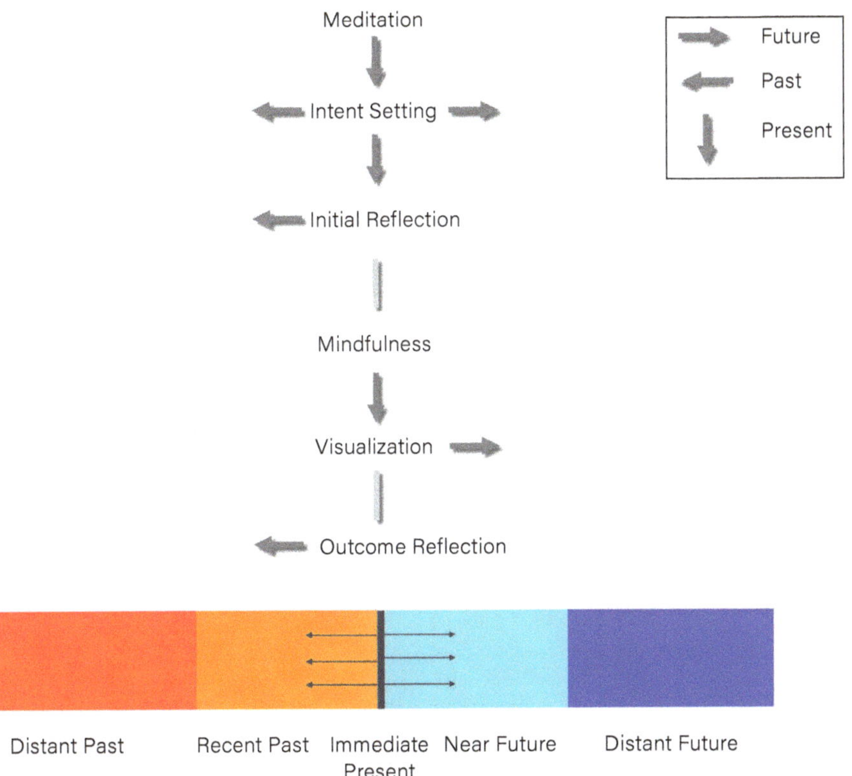

Stage 1: Meditation

We start with Meditation—creating calmness and stillness. Imagine your focus at around a 7 out of 10. It's steady, not too intense, setting the scene for what comes next. Let this calm foundation be your anchor as you explore deeper layers of mindfulness.

"Start steady, let calmness grow, and anchor your mind."

Stage 2: Setting Intent

Next is Intent Setting. Here, your focus softens to around a 5. It's like easing into clarity. Your intention guides your attention, gently shaping your thoughts toward a purpose—whatever feels right in that moment.

"Guide your thoughts with ease."

Stage 3: Insight Reflection: A Check-In

Now comes Insight Reflection. This is your light check-in—a moment to observe thoughts and feelings as they are. Let your focus drop to around a 4. You're just taking a snapshot, not analyzing or changing anything. It's simply noticing.

"Observe. Don't analyze."

Stage 4: Peak Focus with Mindfulness

Then, we move into Mindfulness. Here, your focus peaks around an 8. You're deeply present—fully engaged with your breath, body sensations, and surroundings. This is all about being in the "now," fully connected to the moment.

"Be present. Be here."

Stage 5: Visualize and Imagine

From there, we shift to Visualization. Your focus lightens to about a 6. You're no longer just observing—you're creating an image in your mind. Whether it's peace, balance, or calm, let your visualization fill your awareness, gently guiding your thoughts toward what you want to feel.

"See it. Feel it."

Stage 6: Wrapping Up: Outcome Reflection

Finally, there's Outcome Reflection. Here, your focus eases back down to around a 4. This is a gentle look back, noticing any shifts or insights. It's a mindful close to your practice, leaving you balanced and aware.

"End with calm reflection."

Six Stages of MetaCycle

Stage	Focus Level	Short Description
Meditation	7	Creates calmness and stillness; acts as an anchor.
Setting Intent	5	Softens focus; shapes thoughts with purpose.
Insight Reflection	4	Light check-in; observes thoughts and feelings simply.
Mindfulness	8	Engages deeply with the present; full connection.
Visualization	6	Creates mental imagery; lightens focus on peace or calm.
Outcome Reflection	4	Gently reviews insights; closes with balance.

Why This Flow Matters

The MetaCycle is like a wave—focus gradually rising, peaking, and easing down. This balanced rhythm lets you explore different levels of awareness without feeling overwhelmed. It brings you back to a place of calm and clarity, where you can be both relaxed and fully aware.

"Ride the wave of balance."

Exploring the MetaCycle Layers

The MetaCycle is the heartbeat of OmniMeta Mindfulness, offering two unique rhythms: Macro and Micro. Each layer guides your focus, helping you flow between the broader view of your overall experience and the deeper, more intricate awareness of the present moment.

"Flow between the big and small; find harmony in both."

Exploring the MetaCycle Layers

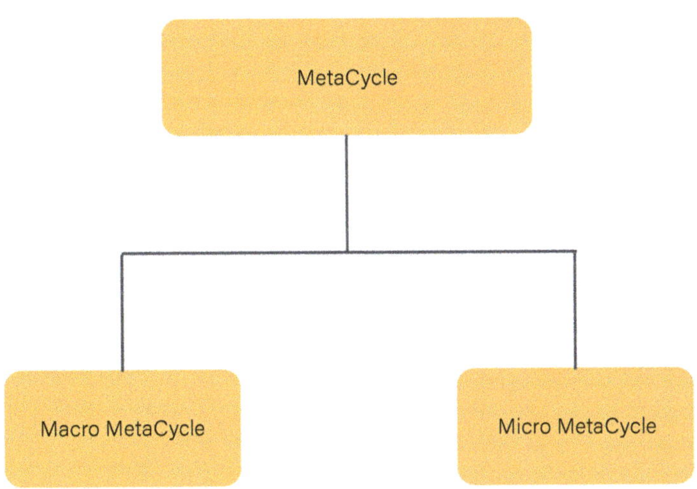

Broadening Perspective with Macro

The Macro MetaCycle gives you the bigger picture—a way to ground yourself and sense the whole experience from start to finish. It's like stepping back to see how everything connects, allowing you to find an overall sense of balance within yourself and your surroundings.

"See the whole, feel the flow."

Zooming In with Micro

Then there's the Micro MetaCycle. Here, we zoom in. It's like taking a magnifying glass to one area—whether it's your body, thoughts, senses, or energy—giving you the chance to observe subtle shifts and sensations. By focusing on these details, you explore each aspect deeply, really getting in touch with yourself.

"Focus on the details that matter."

Finding the Balance: Macro and Micro Together

Together, the Macro and Micro MetaCycles create a balanced flow. You start broad, move into detailed focus, then wrap up with a final reflection. This fluid approach lets you balance seeing the big picture while diving into the finer details—a rhythm that brings wholeness to your practice.

"Balance is the dance between big and small."

MetaCycle Layers

MetaCycle	Description
Macro	Provides a bigger picture, grounding in the overall experience for balance.
Micro	Focuses on details, exploring subtle shifts and sensations deeply.

Notes

Chapter 6

OmniMeta Mindfulness: Six Steps to Balance

The Six Steps of OmniMeta Mindfulness

Let's walk through the six steps of OmniMeta Mindfulness—a guided journey to help you connect more deeply with yourself. Each step is designed to gently bring you closer to awareness, presence, and balance in both your inner world and your day-to-day life.

"Every step inward is a step toward balance."

The Six Steps of OmniMeta Mindfulness

Step Number	Type of Meta	BOSE Element
Step 1	Macro	Warm-Up (Preparation)
Step 2	Micro	Body
Step 3	Micro	Observations
Step 4	Micro	Senses
Step 5	Micro	Energy
Step 6	Macro	Cool Down & Reflection

Step 1: Macro MetaCycle Warm-Up

Begin by tuning into your breath and body, setting a gentle pace to start. This step is all about preparing you for a meaningful practice, helping you find calm, focus, and readiness.

"Breathe in; set the tone."

Step 2: Micro MetaCycle for Body

Shift your attention to your physical self. Gently scan your body from head to toe, noticing areas of tension or relaxation. This check-in strengthens your awareness of how your body feels in the present moment.

"Listen to your body."

Step 3: Micro MetaCycle for Observations

Turn inward to your thoughts and emotions. Notice what's occupying your mind, letting them come and go naturally—no need to fix or change anything. This is your moment to simply be aware.

"See your thoughts, just as they are."

Step 4: Micro MetaCycle for Senses

Tap into your senses—your link to the world around you. Notice what you can hear, see, touch, taste, and smell. Engaging fully with your senses deepens your experience of the present moment.

"Feel the world through your senses."

Step 5: Micro MetaCycle for Energy

Take a moment to check in with your energy. Recognize where your physical, mental, emotional, spiritual, and social energies are active, and notice any areas needing balance. This step tunes you into your natural energy flow.

"Tune into your energy flow."

Step 6: Macro MetaCycle Cool Down & Reflection

Conclude your session with a cool down. Reflect on what you experienced and acknowledge any shifts or changes. Transition back into your day with renewed clarity and balance.

"Reflect and realign."

Bringing It All Together

Each of these steps guides you from broad awareness to focused mindfulness, and then back again. OmniMeta Mindfulness is all about connecting with yourself on a deeper level, finding clarity and presence in your day.

"Awareness. Focus. Balance."

Chapter 7

The Rhythm of OmniMeta Mindfulness

The Unique Flow of OmniMeta Mindfulness

OmniMeta Mindfulness is a refreshing approach to mindfulness. It guides you through different levels of focus, creating a balanced and intentional journey. Each step brings together every part of you—body, mind, senses, and energy—to help you find harmony and balance in your daily life.

"Align body, mind, and spirit."

A Flowing Journey: Like a Melody

Picture it like a melody, not just a single note. You move smoothly through each step—starting with meditation to calm the mind, then setting clear intentions. There's reflection to understand where you are, mindfulness to connect with the moment, and visualization to paint the picture of where you want to go.

"Let your practice flow like music."

Riding the Waves of Focus

Think of this as riding the waves of focus—rising and falling, shifting awareness to different parts of yourself. You're not stuck in one place; you're flowing through the experience, letting each stage naturally lead to the next. The rhythm guides you, gently expanding and contracting your focus.

"Flow through your practice, one wave at a time."

Finding Your Rhythm

It's all about finding that rhythm—where every breath, every thought, every sensation fits and feels like it belongs. With OmniMeta, you'll connect to your whole self, riding those waves toward deeper balance and awareness.

"Find your rhythm, find your balance."

MetaCycle and BOSE Framework Alignment Matrix

Meta Cycle Elements	Step 2 Body	Step 3 Observations	Step 4 Senses	Step 5 Energy
Meditation	Grounding	Awareness	Calmness	Rejuvenation
Intent Setting	Focus	Clarity	Intention	Motivation
Initial Reflection	Relaxation	Insight	Feeling	Balance
Mindfulness	Presence	Observation	Engagement	Connection
Visualization	Imagination	Visualization	Immersion	Empowerment
Outcome Reflection	Review	Understanding	Reflection	Renewal

*This matrix illustrates the relationship between the **Meta Cycle elements** and the core components of the **BOSE Framework**—Body, Observations, Senses, and Energy. Each cell contains a single word that signifies how each Meta Cycle practice engages with one of the BOSE elements. It provides a simplified, clear view of how mindfulness practices in the Meta Cycle connect with physical, mental, sensory, and energetic aspects of mindfulness.*

Chapter 8

OmniMeta as a Mindful Workout

The Mind as a Muscle

Think of your mind like a muscle—it needs both effort and rest to grow stronger. Just like a workout, you don't go all out the whole time; you move through warm-ups, focused exercises, and cool-downs. The MetaCycle follows the same rhythm, guiding your mind to become more flexible, balanced, and strong.

"Flex your focus, build your strength."

Step 1: Warming Up - Meditation

Every workout starts with a warm-up, and so does mindfulness. Meditation is where you set a steady rhythm. You ease into it, gently waking up your mental focus, just like stretching your muscles before you get into the main workout.

"Ease in, find your rhythm."

Step 2: Setting the Intention - Intent Setting

Next is Intent Setting, like planning out your workout session. Here, you set your focus and decide where to channel your mental energy. It's like having a workout plan—you know which areas to target and why.

"Plan your practice, set your intention."

Step 3: Getting in the Groove - Insight Reflection

Now that you're warmed up, it's time to find your groove. Insight Reflection is like those first easy reps at the gym—checking in on how you're feeling. No pressure here, just gentle awareness of your thoughts and emotions, like feeling how your body moves before diving deeper.

"Find your groove, feel your mind."

Step 4: Heavy Lifting - Mindfulness

This is where you go all in. Mindfulness is like hitting your peak in a workout—the intensity is high, and you're fully present. Think of it as lifting weights for your mind, focusing deeply on every thought, breath, and sensation. It builds your mental strength and sharpens your awareness.

"Lift your focus, strengthen your mind."

Step 5: Softening the Focus - Visualization

After the peak of effort, Visualization is like stretching after a tough workout. You let your focus soften, guiding your mind into creative imagery and positive thoughts. It's more than relaxation—it's about intentional relaxation, visualizing balance, and setting your desired outcomes.

"Stretch your mind; see your calm."

Step 6: Final Stretch - Outcome Reflection

Finally, Outcome Reflection is your cool-down stretch—where you take a moment to review and notice how everything came together. Reflect on the shifts or changes you experienced, wrapping up the practice with a calm and grounded finish.

"Reflect on your journey; close with peace."

The Balanced Flow

Each stage of the MetaCycle plays its role, just like every part of a workout. These shifts—warm-up, peak, and cool down—build mental flexibility, clarity, and resilience. It's a total workout for your mind and energy, leaving you refreshed, balanced, and ready for whatever comes next.

"Balance your mind like a workout."

MetaCycle vs. Workout: A Mindful Comparison

Physical Workout Analogy	MetaCycle Step in OmniMeta
Warm-Up Stretch: Light stretching to prepare the body	**Meditation:** Gently ease into practice; find a calm, steady rhythm
Set Workout Goal: Plan your focus for the session	**Intent Setting:** Decide on a mental goal; where to direct focus
Initial Reps: Gentle movements to find your rhythm	**Insight Reflection:** Check in with thoughts & emotions without pressure
Full Effort Exercise: Peak effort, high engagement	**Mindfulness:** Deep focus, present awareness—like lifting weights for the mind
Post-Workout Stretch: Ease into flexibility and relaxation	**Visualization:** Soften focus, explore creative thoughts and intentions
Cool Down & Reflection: Gradual relaxation and reviewing progress	**Outcome Reflection:** Review practice, embrace calmness, and center yourself

Chapter 9

Personal Mastery & Resilience

Building Mental Agility

OmniMeta Mindfulness is about smoothly navigating through different mental states—meditation, reflection, mindfulness, and visualization. This isn't just about staying calm; it's about learning to shift perspectives and refocus your energy when faced with change or stress. These mental "switches" build agility, allowing you to adapt to challenges quickly and find your way back to balance.

"Shift your focus, sharpen your mind."

Flowing Through Change with Flexibility

Every day brings new demands—work deadlines, shifting priorities, emotional ups and downs. OmniMeta helps you build mental flexibility, making it easier to handle whatever life throws your way. With regular practice, you can find your flow—whether it's calming yourself through meditation, bringing clarity through reflection, staying grounded through mindfulness, or sparking creativity through visualization.

"Find your flow; flex with the moment."

Embracing Change, Reducing Resistance

Change can be uncomfortable; resistance is a natural reaction. OmniMeta Mindfulness helps reduce this resistance by promoting a balanced approach. Instead of feeling overwhelmed, you learn to embrace change by shifting perspectives—moving from discomfort to curiosity, from uncertainty to growth. It's about building comfort with the unknown and turning resistance into resilience.

"See change as growth, not a challenge."

Building Mental Strength & Emotional Balance

Much like a workout, OmniMeta trains your mind for resilience and strength. But it's not just about pushing harder—it's about finding the right balance between effort and rest. You learn to manage your energy, staying centered and emotionally steady even in stressful situations. This emotional balance helps you remain clear-headed and focused, without feeling burned out or stretched too thin.

"Balance your effort with ease."

Tapping into Focus, Creativity, and Calm

Life moves fast, and staying steady is key. OmniMeta helps you tap into focus when you need to, creativity when you're stuck, and calm when you're overwhelmed. It's not just about reacting to what's around you—it's about responding thoughtfully. You gain a toolkit to manage life with awareness, finding purpose and creativity in your everyday actions.

"Find clarity, find your spark."

A Practice for the Modern World

Whether you're in a boardroom, a classroom, or anywhere in between, OmniMeta Mindfulness prepares you to navigate the modern world with intention. It gives you the ability to shift gears, adapt quickly, and find balance amidst the noise. Embrace this practice not just to handle change but to thrive in it—with a clear mind, balanced energy, and a sense of purpose.

"Thrive in change; live with intention."

Notes

Chapter 10

Workplace Application & Performance

Everyday Applications of MetaCycle & Mindfulness

OmniMeta Mindfulness and the MetaCycle techniques aren't just about sitting still—they're about building skills that help you thrive in all areas of life, especially in dynamic environments like tech, finance, and business.

"Mindfulness isn't stillness; it's a skill set."

Energy Management for Better Performance

OmniMeta techniques help manage all dimensions of energy—physical, mental, emotional, spiritual, and social. Mastering these energy levels lets you adapt to change, tackle challenges, and keep creativity flowing. It's a toolkit for staying energized, sharp, and ready for innovation.

"Direct your energy; direct your day."

Creativity & Problem-Solving

Creativity is vital in fast-moving industries. Mindfulness enhances your problem-solving skills, letting you think outside the box and spot opportunities others miss. A clear and focused mind paves the way for fresh ideas.

"Clear focus fuels creativity."

Improving Collaboration & Communication

OmniMeta helps you connect deeply with yourself and others. This awareness boosts communication and collaboration—key skills for any team. It fosters empathy, patience, and understanding, which enhances teamwork and bridges gaps in tough conversations.

"Better awareness, better teamwork."

Adaptability & Stress Management

Switching between mental states—like meditation, mindfulness, reflection, and visualization—boosts adaptability. OmniMeta provides tools for handling change calmly, which is particularly helpful when managing tight deadlines and the pressure of rapid growth.

"Adapt to change; manage stress."

Boosting Productivity & Well-Being

Mindfulness and energy management are about maintaining peak productivity without losing your well-being. By tuning into your natural energy rhythms, you can balance focus, creativity, and rest effectively, preventing burnout and promoting long-term success.

"Balance your energy, boost productivity."

Mindfulness as Your Power Move

The power of OmniMeta and MetaCycle lies in their potential to transform how you approach life and work. They become your secret tools for handling challenges, igniting creativity, and staying on top of your game. Make these techniques your power move to transform your work, connections, and personal growth.

"Ready to make mindfulness your power move?"

AUM in OmniMeta Mindfulness

AUM

Before we begin, let's take a moment to introduce AUM—a core part of our OmniMeta Mindfulness practice. AUMis simple yet powerful. For centuries, it's been used to center the mind and focus inward. When you chant it, think of it as a deep, resonant AUM.

"AUM: Center your mind, anchor your focus."

Three states of human consciousness

AUM is a sacred sound symbolizing the three states of human consciousness.

A represents the waking state (external awareness and the material world),

U symbolizes the dream state (inner experiences and imagination), and

M signifies deep sleep or transcendence (beyond conscious thought).

Together, AUM embodies the entire cycle of existence—creation, preservation, and dissolution—while pointing to a higher state of consciousness that transcends all three, symbolizing unity with the universe or the divine.

"Within AUM lies the essence of all that was, is, and will be—uniting the self with the infinite."

The essence of AUM

The essence of AUM lies in its representation of the unity of existence and the harmony of different states of consciousness. It teaches mindfulness in the present moment, encourages embracing inner creativity and dreams, and guides us toward transcending thought to connect with deeper peace. By harmonizing these aspects—awareness, imagination, and transcendence—AUM emphasizes the interconnectedness of life, guiding us toward unity of mind, body, and spirit with the universe. This powerful sound reminds us that all states of being are part of a continuous, interconnected whole.

"AUM is the thread that weaves together the mind, body, and spirit, reminding us of our deep connection with the universe."

The Power of AUM: Feel the Vibration

AUM isn't just a sound—it's a feeling. Chanting AUM calms both your mind and body. Feel the vibration move through you, grounding and focusing your attention. Imagine AUM like a tuning fork, helping you tune out distractions and tune into yourself. It brings you into the present moment, right here, right now.

"Let AUM guide you inward."

AUM in the MetaCycle: A Calming Effect

In OmniMeta Mindfulness, AUM finds its sweet spot during the Meditation Stage of the MetaCycle Essentials—whether you're setting intentions, reflecting, or practicing mindfulness. The rhythm of chanting AUM has a natural calming effect, gently guiding your thoughts to settle and drawing you deeper into your practice.

"AUM: A gentle guide to deeper mindfulness."

Embracing AUM: For Beginners and Beyond

If it's your first time with AUM, no worries—just let the sound, or even the thought of AUM, softly guide you. Feel free to explore how it grounds you, calms you, and brings your awareness inward. Simply let AUM be your anchor, bringing a peaceful focus to your practice.

"Let AUM be your calm."

Chapter 12

AUM Practice

AUM: A Sound of Balance and Connection

AUM is a deep, ancient vibration from Indian tradition. Often called the "sound of the universe," AUM represents unity and harmony. Chanting it helps you center your mind, bringing focus and awareness to the present. Practicing AUM with intention can bring a sense of peace, grounding, and deeper connection to yourself and the world.

"Chant AUM, find your balance."

AUM: The Sound of Centering

AUM is a simple yet powerful chant that helps ground you in meditation. It flows through three parts: starting deep with "A" like 'ahhh,' moving through your chest with "U" like 'oooo,' and ending with a gentle hum of "M" like 'mmmm.' As you chant, exhale naturally, letting the sound resonate for 5-7 seconds. The vibration of AUM brings calm, focus, and connection to your breath and the moment.

"Let AUM flow with your breath."

Feel the Vibration

As you chant, focus on the vibration—like a wave moving from your chest to your lips. Let it ground you, bringing a sense of calm and centering your mind. Feel each vibration draw you deeper inward, connecting you to yourself and the present moment.

"Feel the vibration; find your center."

Pause Between Chants

After each AUM chant, take a few easy breaths in silence. Let the pause soak in the calm the sound creates. Embrace the stillness, allowing the space to bring peace and clarity within.

"In the silence, feel the peace."

Tips for AUMChanting

Keep your shoulders relaxed, and let the sound flow naturally—there's no need to force it. Focus on how the sound feels in your body; let the vibration guide you to a calm state. Sit up straight for deep, smooth breaths, and gently close your lips on the "M" sound to feel that soft hum.

"Breathe easy, let AUM guide you."

What to Avoid

Don't worry about how loud or "perfect" your AUM sounds—just let it happen naturally. Keep your breathing smooth, not holding it too long between chants. And take your time with each part of the —A, U, M—letting them flow seamlessly together.

"No rush, no pressure—just AUM."

Enjoy the Process

AUM chanting is your personal journey, so don't aim for perfection. Just relax, enjoy the process, and let the sound carry you into a peaceful, mindful state. Embrace the journey, and let AUM lead you to calm.

"Enjoy the journey; let AUM find you."

Incorporating AUM into OmniMeta Mindfulness

During MetaCycle Essentials—from Meditation to Visualization—AUM plays a powerful role, especially in the Meditation Stage. Let the sound of AUM help center your focus and quiet your thoughts. Whether you chant it aloud or let it resonate silently within, AUM can guide you to a deeper sense of calm.

"Let AUM guide you inward."

Notes

Chapter 13

AUM Chanting

Step 1: Find Your Posture

Start by finding a comfortable position, either sitting or standing. Make sure your spine is straight, shoulders are relaxed, and chest is open to let your breath flow freely. Adjust your body until you feel both settled and grounded, ready to begin. A comfortable posture makes all the difference in finding your focus.

"Find your balance, sit tall."

Step 2: Take a Deep Breath

Begin with deep, intentional breathing. Slowly inhale through your nose, filling your lungs completely, then exhale gently through your mouth. Repeat this breathing cycle—inhale deeply, exhale slowly. With each breath out, feel any tension leaving your body, letting you settle into a calm state.

"Breathe in peace, breathe out tension."

Step 3: Begin Chanting OM

As you take a deep breath in, prepare to chant AUM on the exhale. Let the sound flow naturally: "Aaaaaa-oooooo-mmmmm." Feel how the vibration starts in your chest and softly hums on your lips as the "M" sound finishes. Allow the sound to resonate deeply throughout your body, bringing your awareness fully into the present moment.

"AUM: Vibrate through every breath."

Step 4: Pause and Reflect

After chanting, take a silent pause. Let your breathing return to its natural rhythm and notice how your body feels. Observe any sensations or shifts in energy, staying relaxed and aware. This moment of stillness is a way to reflect on the impact of the chant.

"In stillness, find reflection."

Step 5: Repeat AUMChanting

Chant AUM again, following the same pattern. Take a deep breath in through your nose, then exhale with the sound: "Aaaaaa-oooooo-mmmmm." Let the vibration carry a wave of calm throughout your entire body, bringing more relaxation with each breath.

"Let AUM carry your calm."

Step 6: Another Silent Pause

Pause once more, breathing naturally. Feel how each exhale relaxes your body deeper, and create space for stillness to grow. Use this pause to reconnect with your breath and let the peace of the practice sink in.

"Pause to feel, pause to breathe."

Step 7: Final AUMChanting

For the last chant, take one deep inhale... then exhale fully with AUM: "Aaaaaa-oooooo-mmmmm." Let this final vibration resonate through your entire being, leaving you with a sense of profound peace and calmness. Each chant builds on the one before, deepening your sense of connection and grounding.

"Resonate with OM; resonate with peace."

Step 8: Rest and Reflect

Finish with a silent rest. Feel the effects of the chanting—the calm, the clarity, and the stillness it brings. Breathe softly, allowing yourself to fully absorb the experience and be present in the moment.

"Breathe in stillness, exhale into clarity."

Closing the Chanting

You've completed your AUM chanting practice. Stay in this peaceful state for a bit longer—either silently repeating AUM in your mind or simply focusing on your breath. Carry this calm energy as you transition into the next part of your day or mindfulness practice.

"Carry peace as you move forward."

OmniMeta Mindfulness Practice

Solid lines represent rigidity, symbolizing the initial resistance to change. As we warm up, we gradually shift from a fixed state to one that is more open and adaptable.

Phase 1

Macro MetaCycle Warm-Up

Before you dive into your OmniMeta Mindfulness practice, it's helpful to kick things off with a Macro MetaCycle warm-up. This warm-up grounds you, balances your body and mind, and gets you ready for the journey ahead. You'll move through these Stages: Meditation, Intent Setting, Insight Reflection, Mindfulness, Visualization, and Outcome Reflection.

"Prepare your mind; prepare your journey."

Step 1: Meditation – Calming Body & Mind

Find a position that feels comfortable—sitting or lying down. Relax your shoulders, lengthen your spine, and gently close your eyes. Breathe deeply through your nose, hold it for a moment, and then slowly exhale through your mouth. Feel each breath pull you deeper into the moment. Let your breath guide you—inhales expanding your chest, exhales softening your body and mind.

"Breathe deeply, settle fully."

Step 2: Intent Setting – Finding Your Focus

Set an intention for your practice, something simple like, "I will be present" or "I'll find peace within." Let this intention shape your session. Each inhale fills you with purpose; each exhale lets go of any pressure for things to be "perfect." Know that whatever comes up today is just right.

"Set an intention, find your focus."

Step 3: Insight Reflection – Checking In

Now, take a moment to see how you're feeling—physically, mentally, and emotionally. Notice sensations in your body, thoughts running through your mind, or any emotions bubbling up. No need to change anything—just observe. Is your body full of energy or feeling tired? Is your mind calm or busy? Use these observations to deepen your awareness.

"Notice without judgment, observe without change."

Step 4: Mindfulness – Being in the Moment

Bring your focus fully to the present. Let your breath be your anchor. Feel the air entering your nose, filling your lungs, and flowing out through your mouth. If your mind starts to wander, gently bring it back to your breath. Let each inhale pull you into the moment, each exhale release any distractions.

"Let each breath bring you back to now."

Step 5: Visualization – Finding Calm & Balance

Shift into visualization. Imagine yourself surrounded by a soft, warm light that brings calm, clarity, and balance. With every inhale, let this light fill your body, creating a sense of peace. As you exhale, picture the light washing away stress or tension, leaving you relaxed and grounded.

"Visualize light; feel balance."

Step 6: Outcome Reflection – Noticing Changes

Take a moment to reflect on how you feel now. Do you sense any shifts—feeling more centered, balanced, or aware of your breath and body? Recognize your experience with gratitude for the calm and clarity you've cultivated. Appreciate this time of self-awareness.

"Recognize your calm; reflect on your journey."

Closing – Transition to the BOSE Framework

You've completed the Macro MetaCycle warm-up—a strong start to build mindfulness into your practice. Take a final deep breath in... and as you exhale, feel present and ready. Bring this sense of calm and balance as you move into the BOSE Framework. You're grounded, centered, and ready for what's next.

"Grounded in calm, ready for the next step."

Notes

Phase 2

Micro Meta Scan for the Body

Using the MetaCycle, we shift our focus to the body—the first element of the BOSE Framework. The Micro Meta Scan guides you to connect deeply with your physical state, step by step.

"Connect with your body; find your center."

Step 1: Meditation – Calming the Body

Start by calming down. Take a deep breath in... then slowly let it out. Feel your body relax as it's supported by whatever you're sitting or lying on. Allow yourself to rest and bring your attention inward. Notice your breath and how your body feels in this moment.

"Breathe in stillness, breathe out calm."

Step 2: Intent Setting – Creating Your Focus

Set a simple intention for this scan. It could be to release any tension, bring attention to any discomfort, or just notice how your body feels without judgment. Let this intention be your guide throughout the practice.

"Set your intention, guide your focus."

Step 3: Insight Reflection – Checking In with Your Body

Now, check in with your body. Notice how you feel without trying to change anything. Are there places that feel tight or relaxed? Does your body feel tense or at ease? Use this moment to assess your current physical state and observe any sensations.

"Observe your body; notice what is."

Step 4: Mindfulness – Scanning the Body

Gently scan your body from head to toe. Start with your head—notice any tension without trying to fix it. Move down to your face: your jaw, forehead, and eyes. Breathe into any tightness you notice. Then shift to your neck and shoulders, feeling into these areas. Continue down to your arms, hands, chest, stomach, back, hips, legs, and feet. Tune into how each area feels.

"Scan your body; tune into every sensation."

Step 5: Visualization – Projecting Comfort

Visualize your body in its most relaxed state—balanced, free of tension, and at ease. Imagine your shoulders dropping, your face softening, and your whole body aligning harmoniously. Let this image of comfort and relaxation fill every part of you.

"See your body as relaxed; feel it at ease."

Step 6: Outcome Reflection – Recognizing Changes

Take a moment to reflect on how your body feels now. Do you notice any changes? Are you feeling more relaxed or comfortable? Compare how you feel now to when you began, and appreciate any shifts toward balance.

"Notice the changes; feel the balance."

Completing the Micro Meta Scan

You've just completed a Micro Meta Scan for your body using the MetaCycle. Each step has helped you connect, adjust, and find comfort. Take one last deep breath in... and slowly let it out. When you're ready, move on to the next element in the BOSE Framework.

"Connect, breathe, move forward."

Notes

Phase 3

Micro Meta Scan for Observations

The Micro Meta Scan for Observations focuses on tuning into your thoughts, emotions, and surroundings. It's about checking in with your mental and emotional state in the present moment. Let your awareness flow naturally as you move through the MetaCycle.

"Observe your thoughts; connect with your emotions."

Step 1: Meditation – Calming the Mind

Start by finding a comfortable spot to sit or lie down. Close your eyes if it feels right. Take a deep breath in through your nose... and gently breathe out through your mouth. With each breath, let your body relax and your mind settle, making space for the here and now.

"Breathe in stillness; exhale mental clutter."

Step 2: Intent Setting – Focus for Observations

With a calm mind, set a light intention for this practice. It might be something like "I'll observe my emotions" or "I'll notice my thoughts without judgment." Let this intention guide your awareness gently, keeping you centered as you explore your thoughts and feelings.

"Set a light intention; focus without judgment."

Step 3: Insight Reflection – Checking In

Take a moment to reflect on how you're feeling mentally and emotionally. Notice any recurring thoughts or standout feelings. Is your mind scattered or still? Calm or racing? You don't need to analyze—just notice what's happening within.

"Reflect without analyzing; observe without changing."

Step 4: Mindfulness – Awareness of Thoughts & Surroundings

Now, anchor yourself in the present. Use your breath to ground you. Notice how your thoughts move—are they steady or jumping around? Let them flow without trying to control them. If your attention drifts, gently bring it back to your breath. Be aware of any sounds, sensations, or the environment around you.

"Let your breath anchor you to now."

Step 5: Visualization – Projecting Calm & Clarity

Visualize your mind as a calm, clear space—like a still lake with passing clouds representing your thoughts and emotions. Imagine yourself in a peaceful setting, feeling grounded. Let your thoughts settle and your emotions ease, filling your mind with clarity and peace.

"See your thoughts drift; feel your mind clear."

Step 6: Outcome Reflection – Noticing Shifts

Reflect on how you feel now. Does your mind feel clearer, more at ease? Are you more aware of your emotions? Without diving too deep, simply acknowledge any shifts or changes in your mental state. Appreciate this moment of awareness and calm.

"Recognize your clarity; honor your awareness."

Closing – Embracing Calm & Mindfulness

You've completed a Micro Meta Scan for Observations. By tuning into your thoughts, emotions, and environment, you've gained a deeper sense of presence. Carry this mindful clarity with you throughout your day. Take one deep breath in... and gently let it go.

"Carry clarity; move with calm."

Notes

Phase 4

Micro Meta Scan for Senses

Now let's focus on the third part of the BOSE Framework—Senses. Our senses connect us to the world, and this practice is all about tuning into what you're experiencing through sight, sound, touch, taste, and smell. A Micro Meta Scan will guide you to be more aware of all the sensory details around you.

"Let your senses connect you to the moment."

Step 1: Meditation – Calming the Body & Mind

Find a comfy position to sit. If it feels right, gently close your eyes. Take a deep breath in through your nose... and out through your mouth. With every breath, release any tension and allow your body to find stillness, bringing your attention inward and calming the mind.

"Breathe in stillness; breathe out tension."

Step 2: Intent Setting – Tuning into Your Senses

With your mind settled, set an intention—like simply being more aware of your senses. Allow yourself to observe without judgment. Let this intention be your gentle guide as you breathe, staying open to every sensation.

"Tune into the world; observe without judgment."

Step 3: Insight Reflection – Observing Your Sensory Experience

Tune into what your senses are picking up. Start by listening—what sounds are around you? Notice them, whether they're soft, loud, near, or far. Then bring attention to touch—how does the air feel on your skin? How does your body rest against the floor or chair?

"Listen to the world, feel its touch."

Step 4: Mindfulness – Present Awareness of Your Senses

Bring full attention to each sense, one at a time. Listen deeply—hear your breath, any distant noises, or silence. Feel—notice your clothing, your body resting, the air's warmth or coolness. Smell—take a breath and notice any faint or strong scents. Taste—observe any flavor lingering in your mouth. And finally, sight—whether your eyes are closed or open, notice colors, shapes, light, and shadows around you.

"Notice each sense; be fully present."

Step 5: Visualization – Enhancing Sensory Clarity

Imagine each of your senses becoming sharper. Visualize your hearing more attuned, your touch more aware, your vision brighter. Picture yourself deeply in tune with your surroundings, each sense clear and connected.

"Visualize clarity; feel every sensation."

Step 6: Outcome Reflection – Noticing Sensory Shifts

Reflect on any shifts in your sensory awareness. Are sounds clearer? Is your body more sensitive to touch? Notice how your senses feel now compared to when you started. Appreciate the awareness and clarity you've cultivated.

"Reflect on the senses; honor your clarity."

Closing – Carrying Sensory Awareness

You've completed the Micro Meta Scan for Senses. By paying mindful attention to hearing, touch, smell, taste, and sight, you've deepened your connection to the moment. Let this heightened sensory awareness stay with you as you go about your day.

"Breathe in clarity; exhale connection."

Notes

Phase 5

Micro Meta Scan for Energy

In this practice, we'll focus on the Energy element of the BOSE Framework. We'll explore different types of energy—physical, mental, emotional, spiritual, and social. The goal is to become aware of how each type feels in the moment and how your energy flows throughout your day.

"Tune into your energy; feel its flow."

Step 1: Meditation – Calming Mind & Body

Find a comfortable seated position, keeping your spine straight and your hands resting gently. Close your eyes and take a deep breath in... then exhale slowly. Feel your body relax as you let your breath find its natural rhythm, releasing tension with each exhale. As your body settles, prepare to tune into your energy.

"Breathe in calm; exhale tension."

Step 2: Intent Setting – Tuning into Your Energy

Now that you're feeling calm, set a gentle intention. This could be to explore how your energy feels, to notice any imbalances, or to connect more deeply with yourself. Think of this as planting a seed of purpose. With each inhale, bring this intention to mind, and as you exhale, let it settle gently.

"Set your intention; let your energy guide you."

Step 3: Insight Reflection – Noticing Current Energy Levels

Reflect on your energy, starting with the physical. On a scale from 1 to 5, where 1 is low and 5 is fully energized, how would you rate your physical energy? Are you feeling active, tired, or somewhere in between? Next, shift to your mental energy. How clear and focused is your mind? Is it sharp, scattered, or somewhere in between? Just notice where your mental energy stands.

"Notice without judgment; observe your flow."

Step 4: Mindfulness – Exploring Each Energy Type

Explore each type of energy mindfully. Start with physical energy—observe how your body feels. Is there tension or relaxation, heaviness or lightness? Rate your awareness of these physical sensations on a scale of 1 to 5.

Move to mental energy. Are your thoughts steady or racing? Focused or wandering? Rate your mental clarity.

Next, focus on your emotional energy. Are you calm, content, or restless? How are your emotions shaping your energy? Rate your emotional state.

Then, consider your spiritual energy—how connected do you feel to yourself or something greater? Are you aligned or disconnected? Notice how this spiritual energy feels and rate it.

Finally, reflect on your social energy. How have recent interactions impacted you? Do you feel uplifted or drained? Acknowledge how these connections affect you and rate them.

"Explore deeply; let your awareness flow."

Step 5: Visualization – Balancing & Restoring Energy

Visualize all types of energy flowing smoothly—balanced and harmonious. Picture your physical energy as strong, your mental energy as clear, your emotional energy as calm, your spiritual energy as deeply connected, and your social energy as positive. Imagine all these energies working together to support and balance each other.

"See your energy balance; feel your harmony."

Step 6: Outcome Reflection – Noticing Energy Shifts

Reflect on any shifts in your energy. Have your ratings changed? Do you feel more balanced, grounded, or aware? Just observe any changes in your physical, mental, emotional, spiritual, or social energy since you started this practice.

"Observe the shifts; embrace your balance."

Closing – Carrying Energy Awareness

You've completed the Micro Meta Scan for Energy. By connecting with each type of energy, you've gained a deeper understanding of your present state. Carry this balance and awareness with you throughout your day. Take a final deep breath in... and gently exhale, feeling centered and balanced.

"Breathe in balance; exhale awareness."

Notes

Dotted lines represent fluidity and adaptability. During cool down, we transition into a flexible, open state, ready to embrace change and release the intensity, preparing for future challenges with ease.

Phase 6

Closing the OmniMeta Mindfulness Session

Congratulations! You've successfully completed the Micro Meta Scan for all four elements of the BOSE Framework: Body, Observations, Senses, and Energy. Throughout this journey, you've explored different layers of your being—both internally and externally. You've tuned into how your body feels, how your mind thinks, how your senses perceive, and how your energy flows.

"Inhale mindfulness, exhale awareness."

Settling into Calm & Clarity

Take a deep breath in... and slowly release it. Allow your awareness to settle into the calm and clarity you've cultivated during this session. You've taken the time to be present with yourself; now let this sense of balance support you as you move through your day.

"Breathe in balance, breathe out peace."

Reflecting on Shifts

Take a moment to notice how you're feeling now compared to when we started. Do you feel more grounded, relaxed, or energized? There's no right or wrong response—just observe how this practice has impacted your awareness and energy levels.

"Observe the shift; embrace the balance."

Reconnecting with Your Surroundings

Gently begin to bring your awareness back to your surroundings. If your eyes are closed, slowly open them, allowing the light and colors to come into focus. Feel the surface beneath you—the chair or floor—and reconnect with the space around you.

"See the world anew, through mindful eyes."

Taking Mindfulness with You

Remember, the mindfulness you've cultivated doesn't have to end here. Carry this clarity and balance with you as you navigate work, rest, or social connections. Take one last deep breath in... and as you exhale, release any remaining tension.

"Carry calm; let mindfulness guide you."

Closing & Gratitude

You've completed a full session of OmniMeta Mindfulness. Take a moment to appreciate yourself for dedicating this time to nurture your body, mind, and energy. When you feel ready, gently rise or move forward, feeling centered and balanced, ready to embrace the rest of your day.

"Move with balance; live with presence."

Chapter 15

Yoga Practice for Relaxation

Mudra Pose

Gentle Yoga Session

This yoga session emphasizes gentle breathing and movements designed to help you stretch, relax, and re-energize—all from the comfort of your home. We'll begin with a calming breathing exercise, then transition into soothing postures to ease your body and mind.

"Breathe in peace, breathe out tension."

Exercise 1

Dirga Pranayama (Three-Part Breath):

Start with Dirga Pranayama (Three-Part Breath). This technique calms the mind, reduces stress, and increases lung capacity, bringing balance to your body. Find a comfortable seated position with your back straight. Close your eyes if it feels natural. Place one hand on your belly and the other on your chest to feel the breath move through your body.

"Feel each breath, connect with yourself."

Practicing the Three-Part Breath (5 times)

Take a deep breath in through your nose, allowing the air to fill your belly first, then expand into your ribcage, and finally rise to your chest. Exhale slowly, releasing air from your chest, then your ribcage, and finally your belly. Continue this breath cycle five times—slowly and mindfully. Feel each inhale bring calm, and each exhale melt away tension.

"Inhale deeply, exhale stress."

Benefits of Dirga Pranayama

This breathing exercise soothes your nervous system, promotes relaxation, and enhances lung capacity. As you breathe deeply and fully, notice how it shifts your energy, helping you feel more centered and at ease.

"Breathe fully, find your calm."

Moving Forward

Now that your breath is centered and your mind is calm, you're ready to transition to the next part of the session. Let your breath guide you, creating a gentle flow from one movement to the next. Take your time, enjoy the process, and carry this sense of ease as you move forward.

"Let your breath lead your practice."

Notes

Exercise 2

Anulom Vilom (Alternate Nostril Breathing)**:**

Finding Balance with Breath

Anulom Vilom—also known as Alternate Nostril Breathing—is all about balance. This simple technique helps calm your mind, improve focus, and promote a sense of equilibrium.

"Balance your breath, balance your mind."

Setting Up Your Posture

Find a comfortable seated position with a straight spine and relaxed shoulders. Rest your left hand on your knee, palm facing up, and use your right hand to guide your breath throughout the practice.

"Sit tall, breathe easy."

Practicing the Breath Flow (10 Rounds)

1. Gently close your right nostril with your right thumb.

2. Inhale slowly through your left nostril, filling your lungs with air.

3. Close your left nostril with your right ring finger, release your thumb, and exhale through the right nostril.

4. Inhale deeply through the right nostril.

5. Close the right nostril again with your thumb, release your ring finger from the left, and exhale through the left nostril.

Repeat this flow for 10 rounds, letting each breath bring balance and calmness to your mind and body.

"Inhale peace, exhale tension."

Benefits of Anulom Vilom

This breathing practice helps balance both hemispheres of the brain, enhances focus, reduces stress, and calms the nervous system. Feel the soothing rhythm of your breath, bringing harmony and clarity.

"A balanced breath creates a balanced life."

Transitioning with Calm Energy

Take a moment to notice the effects of this breathwork—the sense of relaxation and centeredness it brings. Let this balanced energy carry you smoothly into the next part of your practice.

"Breathe in harmony, breathe out balance."

Exercise 3

Kapalbhati (Skull Shining Breath)**:**

Energize & Detoxify

Kapalbhati, or Skull Shining Breath, is an energizing practice that detoxifies your body, boosts your energy, and strengthens your core. It's a great way to wake up both your mind and body, bringing clarity and focus to your day.

"Let your breath spark energy from within."

Preparing for Kapalbhati

Sit comfortably with your spine straight, shoulders relaxed. Rest your hands on your knees with palms facing down. Gently close your eyes or lower your gaze to help you focus.

"Sit tall, breathe bright."

The Practice: Sharp & Active Breathing (Time: 1-2 minutes per round)

1. Inhale deeply through your nose.

2. Exhale forcefully through your nose, pulling your belly inward toward your spine. Focus on strong, quick exhales; inhales will happen naturally.

"Exhale with strength, inhale with ease."

Round 1: 30 Sharp Breaths

Start with 30 quick exhales, focusing on pushing each breath out forcefully. Keep your awareness on your belly's movement as you breathe.

"Each exhale clears the mind, each inhale recharges."

Pause & Rest (Time: 30 seconds)

After 30 breaths, let your breathing return to its natural rhythm. Relax and notice the effects—feel the energy flowing and the sense of calm settling in.

"Find stillness in your breath; feel the calm within."

Round 2: Boost the Energy Again

Ready for another round? Take another set of 30 sharp exhales, maintaining focus on your breath. Feel the buildup of energy as your body recharges.

"With every breath, feel the power within."

The Benefits of Kapalbhati

Kapalbhati releases toxins, increases overall energy, and tones your abdominal muscles. It's a powerful practice to invigorate both body and mind.

"Breathe out the old, breathe in the new."

Carrying the Energy Forward

Breathe naturally for a moment, noticing the clarity and warmth flowing through you. Let's carry this renewed energy into the next part of your practice.

"Feel the vitality in every breath."

Notes

Exercise 4

Bhramari (Bee Breath):

Humming to Calm

Bhramari, or Bee Breath, is a soothing practice that helps release tension, reduce stress, and sharpen your focus. It's a simple technique where a gentle hum resonates through your body, creating a sense of deep peace and calm.

"Let your breath hum its way to calm."

Preparing for Bhramari

Sit comfortably with your spine straight. Bring your hands up and place your index fingers gently on the cartilage of your ears, where you can press to partially close the ear canal.

"Find your calm, sit tall."

The Practice: The Gentle Hum (Time: 2-3 minutes)

1. Close your eyes and take a deep breath in.

2. As you exhale, create a soft humming sound, like a buzzing bee.

3. Allow the hum to flow naturally, letting the vibrations fill your head and chest.

"Feel the hum; let it carry away tension."

Continue for 5 Rounds

Inhale deeply, then hum as you exhale. Repeat this for 5 rounds, maintaining a gentle, steady hum. Notice how the vibrations soothe your senses, bringing a deeper sense of calmness with each breath.

"Vibrate calmness through every breath."

The Benefits of Bhramari

Bhramari activates your parasympathetic nervous system, helping to reduce anxiety, calm your nerves, and promote relaxation. It's like pressing a reset button for your mind.

"Hum your way to inner peace."

Carrying the Calm Forward

You've completed your Bhramari practice. Let this peaceful, relaxed energy guide you through the rest of your day or into your next practice.

"Let the hum linger as a quiet sense of ease."

Notes

Exercise 5

Baddha Konasana (Butterfly Pose):

Opening the Hips

Baddha Konasana, or Butterfly Pose, is a gentle stretch that helps release tension in your hips, stretch your inner thighs, and improve flexibility. It's like giving your lower body a soft wake-up call.

"Let your hips open like butterfly wings."

Getting Into Butterfly Pose

Bring the soles of your feet together, allowing your knees to drop to the sides like wings. Hold your feet with both hands, and sit up tall, lengthening through your spine.

"Sit tall, find your balance."

First Round: Gentle Flaps (Time: 30 seconds)

Gently flap your knees up and down like a butterfly in flight. Aim for 4-5 soft flaps every 10 seconds. Breathe in as you lengthen your spine, and breathe out as your knees gently lower toward the floor.

"Breathe in length, breathe out openness."

Rest & Reflect (Time: 10 seconds)

Take a short break. Let your legs relax naturally, and breathe deeply, feeling a soft stretch through your hips. Allow any tension to melt away as you settle into the moment.

"Pause, breathe, and let the tension release."

Second Round: Deeper Movement (Time: 30 seconds)

Flap your knees for another 30 seconds, keeping the same gentle rhythm. Let each breath guide your movement—inhale to lengthen your spine, and exhale as your knees lower a little more toward the floor.

"With each flap, find more space in your hips."

Benefits of Baddha Konasana

This pose helps open up your hips, improves flexibility, and gently releases tightness in your lower body.

"Release tightness, welcome flexibility."

Closing the Pose (Time: 30 seconds)

Take a few final deep breaths. Slowly bring your knees together, and take a moment to notice the new lightness and openness in your hips.

"Embrace the openness; carry it with you."

Exercise 6

Padtanguli Naman & Janu Naman (Toe Stretch and Knee Squeeze):

Releasing Tension in the Legs

Loosen up your legs and feet with gentle stretches and rolls. These simple moves help ease tension, improve flexibility, and boost circulation.

"Stretch, roll, and relax your way to ease."

Stretching Your Toes (Time: 1 minute)

Sit comfortably with your legs straight in front of you. Point your toes forward to feel the stretch across the tops of your feet. Then flex your toes back toward your body to stretch through your calves and the bottoms of your feet.

"Feel the stretch, from toes to calves."

Rotate Your Ankles (Time: 1 minute)

After a few rounds of pointing and flexing, rotate your feet together—first clockwise, then counterclockwise. Move slowly, like you're drawing circles with your toes, and let your ankles loosen up.

"Feel the release as you gently move your feet."

Adding Knee Rolls (Time: 30 seconds)

With your legs still extended, softly squeeze your knees, then release. This gentle movement helps relax your knee joints and leg muscles.

"Squeeze and release for soft knees."

Repeat for Relaxation (Time: 2-3 minutes)

Go through the sequence again—pointing and flexing your toes, rotating your ankles, and rolling your knees. Notice how each round brings more lightness and relaxation to your legs.

"Find lightness in each gentle stretch and roll."

Benefits of Padtanguli Naman & Janu Naman

These movements improve blood circulation, relax tight muscles, and support flexibility in your legs and feet.

"Move freely, let circulation flow."

Closing the Stretch (Time: 30 seconds)

Take a final moment to stretch and relax your legs and feet. When ready, bring your legs back to a comfortable position, feeling the newfound ease and flexibility.

"Flexibility comes with gentle attention."

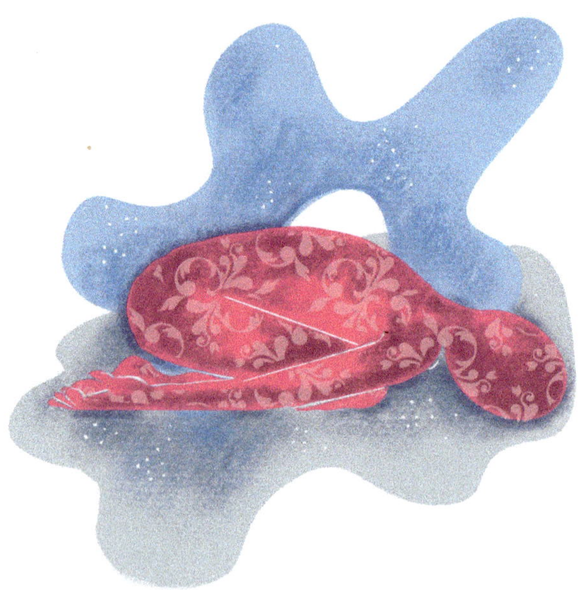

Exercise 7

Balasana (Child's Pose):

A Restful Stretch for Back and Hips

Balasana, or Child's Pose, is a soothing way to release tension in your back and hips, bringing a sense of calm and grounding to your practice.

Settling into the Pose

Sit back on your heels with your big toes touching. Your knees can be together or spread wide—whatever feels more comfortable for you. As you exhale, gently fold forward from your hips, bringing your forehead to the ground. If that's not comfy, rest it on a block or pillow. Extend your arms forward, palms down, and let your fingers naturally reach out.

"Breathe in calm; breathe out tension."

Softening and Stretching (Time: 1-3 minutes)

Let your body relax into the pose. Allow your belly to rest between your thighs and your chest to soften toward the floor. Breathe deeply—inhaling through your nose, exhaling through your mouth. Feel the gentle stretch along your spine and into your hips. With each exhale, imagine the tension melting away. Let your shoulders, hips, and fingers release as the floor supports you.

"With every breath, melt into ease."

Benefits of Balasana (Child's Pose)

This pose gently stretches the spine, relaxes your entire body, and reduces fatigue and stress. It helps you reconnect with your breath and find a sense of ease.

"Find rest in stillness, and ease in every breath."

Staying Present (Time: 2-3 minutes)

Take a few more breaths, finding comfort and stillness. If it feels good, gently sway your hips side to side, or stay still and allow your breath to guide you deeper into the stretch. When you're ready, slowly rise, lifting your chest to a seated position. Move gently, carrying this calm into the rest of your practice.

"Pause, relax, and let go."

Exercise 8

Savasana (Corpse Pose):

The Art of Relaxation

Savasana, or Corpse Pose, is all about letting go, deeply relaxing, and finding balance. It's a moment to reset your body and mind, allowing you to fully absorb your practice.

Getting Comfortable (Time: 5-10 minutes)

Lie flat on your back. Let your legs fall open naturally, feet about hip-width apart, and toes relaxed to the sides. Rest your arms slightly away from your body, palms facing up. Adjust yourself until you feel totally at ease—tuck your shoulder blades, place a pillow under your knees, or wrap yourself in a blanket if that feels right.

"Relax, release, renew."

Melt into Relaxation

Gently close your eyes and allow your body to soften. Feel your face relax, unclench your jaw, and let your shoulders sink down. Let your breath flow softly—inhale through your nose, exhale through your mouth. With every exhale, feel your body getting heavier, surrendering to the floor beneath you.

"With every breath, sink deeper into stillness."

Letting Go

In Savasana, let go of any thoughts, worries, or to-do lists. Imagine each breath carrying away tension and leaving only calm and stillness. Allow your whole body to soak up the benefits of your practice, restoring your energy and finding deep relaxation.

"Exhale your worries, inhale your peace."

The Benefits of Savasana

Savasana is like hitting the reset button—helping to recharge your energy, promote deep relaxation, and calm both mind and body. It's a peaceful moment to re-center and recharge.

"Reset, recharge, and let tranquility renew your spirit."

Slowly Reawaken

When you're ready to come back, start by wiggling your fingers and toes. Rotate your wrists and ankles, and stretch your arms overhead like you're waking up from a great sleep. Roll gently to one side, using your arm as a pillow, and take a breath. Then, when you're ready, gently push yourself up to a seated position.

Take a final deep breath in, and as you exhale, thank yourself for this time of self-care and mindfulness.

"Embrace the calm and carry it with you."

Closing Your Yoga Session

As you wrap up your session, gently start to wake up your body. Wiggle your fingers and toes, feeling the subtle movements bringing you back. Slowly, like a soft morning stretch, let your awareness return to the space around you.

"Awaken gently, bringing calm from practice into presence."

Transition to a Seated Pose (Time: 1-2 minutes)

When you're ready, roll over to one side, letting your head rest on your arm. Take a calming breath here, staying in this relaxed state for a moment longer. Gently push yourself up into a comfortable seated position—cross your legs if that feels good, and rest your hands on your knees or lap. Sit tall, lengthening your spine, and allow your shoulders to soften.

"Awaken with ease, rise with calm."

Final Centering Breath

Close your session with a centering breath. Inhale deeply through your nose, letting your chest rise and your spine grow tall. Exhale completely, releasing any leftover tension and feeling grounded and at peace.

"Breathe in strength, exhale peace—find your center."

Completing Your Practice

Well done—you've completed your yoga session. I hope you leave feeling more balanced, relaxed, and ready for whatever comes next. Remember, this practice is here for you anytime you need a moment to breathe, stretch, and reconnect.

"Breathe in balance; breathe out peace."

With gratitude and calm, carry this peaceful energy with you throughout your day.

Namaste!

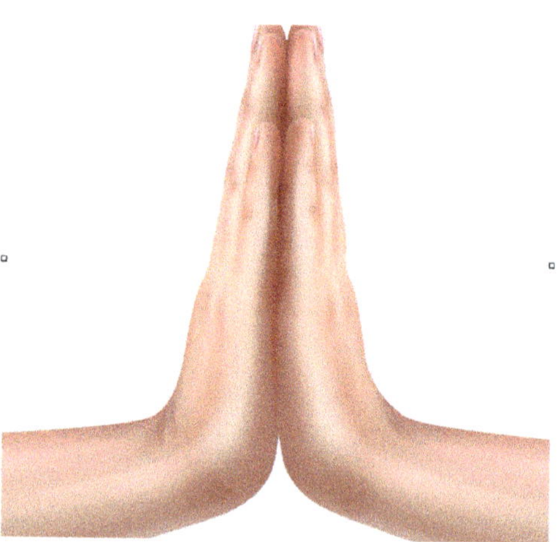